I0457895

Mind is the Matter
And YOU Matter!

Eric F Gilbert

ISBN: 978-1-968365-10-3

0

Dedication

For everyone still fighting battles no one

else can see.

You are stronger than you know.

It's not Mind over matter,

Mind is the matter — and YOU matter.

Table of Contents

Preface

I am not a licensed therapist.
I am not a counselor.
I am not a doctor.

What I am is someone who has been hurt by trauma and has struggled with mental illness for as long as I can remember.

I know firsthand what it feels like to fight battles that no one else can see. I know the pain that comes not only from what's happening inside your own mind but also from the broken relationships and missed opportunities that mental illness can leave in its wake.

I also know firsthand how powerful therapy and professional help can be. Getting the right help can change your life. It changed mine.

This book is not written from a clinical perspective. It's written from the trenches, from the real world. From someone who has lived it, survived it, and—by most standards—succeeded in life, even while carrying invisible battles every day.

My friends are successful business owners, multimillionaires, and even a few billionaires. In their eyes, and in the eyes of most people who meet me, I am a symbol of success. I've built and sold businesses. I've built a life that many would admire.

But what most people don't see are the dark secrets that haunt me. They don't see the nights spent wrestling with demons that no amount of money or success could silence. They don't see the scars hidden beneath the surface.

That's why I wrote this book.

Not because I have all the answers.
Not because I'm perfect.
But because I've lived it—and because I know that if you're still breathing, you're still winning.

If you're struggling right now, hear me:
You are not broken beyond repair.
You are not alone.
And your best days aren't behind you—they're still out there waiting.

This book is a map built from scars. It's a collection of the truths, mindsets, and tools that helped me keep standing when everything in me wanted to fall.

If even one page helps you hold on a little longer, fight a little harder, or believe in yourself a little more—it's worth it.

Mind is the matter.
And you are stronger than you think.

Introduction: Why This Book Exists

I never thought I'd be writing this book.
Truthfully, today is a low day for me.
And maybe that's exactly why this book matters.

I'm not here to ask for your sympathy. I'm not here to lay out a tragedy and call it inspiration. I'm just here to tell you the truth: life can get brutal, and some days, surviving is success.

When I was six years old, something happened that I didn't know how to process. I was sexually abused—something no child should ever endure. I didn't tell anyone. I didn't even allow myself to admit it had happened. Threatened into silence, I did the only thing my mind knew to do: I dissociated. I pushed it so deep that for decades, I honestly believed it hadn't happened.

I grew up carrying a pain I couldn't name. Depression followed me like a shadow, and thoughts of suicide began haunting me as early as twelve years old. But somehow, I convinced myself that I was "strong enough" to handle it alone. Therapy, medication, even asking for help—they weren't even considerations. I thought strength meant silence. I thought surviving meant pretending.

My first two marriages ended after their
infidelity. They weren't easy marriages to begin
with, but each collapse drove another crack into
my already fragile sense of self. When my third
marriage immediately fell apart, I couldn't deny it
anymore:
The common denominator was me.

Finally, in my late forties, I walked into therapy. I
don't know why it took me so long. Maybe
stubbornness. Maybe fear. Maybe just never
having a model for what real healing could look
like.

It was in one of those early sessions that my
therapist asked if I had ever been abused. I told
her no—because, in my mind, I hadn't.
But she saw something I couldn't see yet. She
saw the markers of deep, buried trauma.

She asked if I would take a questionnaire. Three
questions in, the dam broke. Every memory I had
fought so hard to bury came flooding back all at
once. It was horrifying. It was disorienting. It was
the beginning of finally, truly understanding
myself.

The reality was brutal:
I had been dissociating since I was six years old.

The last real, connected memories I had—the last things I could remember truly enjoying— were from when I was a child.

Imagine waking up in your late forties and realizing you had been living half-asleep for forty years.

It got even stranger.
A few days after the memories returned, the person who had hurt me reached out and asked if they had ever done anything to me as a child that they needed forgiveness for.
At that point, I was still too numb to even process it.
I brushed it off.
Later, when I tried to open the door for real healing, they got angry and cut me off completely.

The thing about trauma is that it doesn't stay politely tucked away in the past.
It bleeds into your relationships.
It buries itself in your decisions.
It writes on your heart when you're not even looking.

It was the root of my lifelong battles with depression.
It was the unseen chain pulling at my marriages, my relationship with my kids, my nights haunted

by terrors so violent I have to take pills just to be able to sleep, and more pills to keep from thrashing out and hitting my wife in sleep.

Eventually, I was diagnosed with Bipolar II disorder—a diagnosis that finally explained the highs and devastating lows that had colored my life for as long as I could remember.

But here's the part that matters:
None of it has stopped me.

Most people who know me don't know this story.
Very few do.
Because my life isn't a sob story—it's a victory story still being written.

I'm still standing.
I'm still building.
I'm still reaching.
And if you're reading this, so are you.

This book isn't about what happened to me.
I know that I'm not alone in this. I have friends and family that have suffered just as horrible things or worse than I have.

It's about what's happening now:
The fight to keep going, even on the days when it would be easier to give up.

If today is a low day for you, know that you're not alone.
You're not broken beyond repair.
You're not hopeless.

This is a book for the fighters.
For the people who keep showing up, even when their mind tries to convince them not to.
For the ones who don't need another motivational poster—they just need someone to tell them the truth and to walk beside them one more day.

Mind is the matter.
And you are stronger than you think.

Chapter 1: The Hidden Battles We Carry

Pain doesn't make an appointment. It just shows up.
And for many of us, it shows up early.

The facts are brutal:
According to the National Child Traumatic Stress Network, nearly 78% of children reported more than one traumatic experience before the age of 5. Trauma is common. It's not rare. And for those of us who experience it young, it plants roots that reach far into adulthood.

Trauma doesn't just live in your memory. It rewires your brain.
Studies show that early childhood trauma can physically change the structure of the brain, impacting everything from emotional regulation to decision-making to self-worth.

If you've struggled, it's not because you're weak. It's because your mind was forced to survive something before it was ever ready.

You don't fix a broken foundation by painting the walls. You rebuild from the ground up.

When my battle began, I didn't even recognize it as a battle.
At six years old, I didn't have the language to name trauma.
I only knew that part of me went missing.

And that's often how it starts:
Not with a moment of obvious disaster, but with a slow erosion of identity.
You become a stranger to yourself without even realizing it.

The Silent Symptoms

For decades, I carried silent symptoms:

Depression that felt like it had no beginning and no end.

Anxiety that wrapped itself around normal life like a chokehold.

Dissociation so deep I didn't even realize I was dissociating.

Thoughts of suicide as early as twelve years old, normalized in my mind as "just the way life is."

The American Foundation for Suicide Prevention reports that suicide is the 11th leading cause of

death in the United States, and that over 12 million American adults seriously think about suicide each year.
You are not strange for struggling.
You are not alone in the fight.

The Myth of Strength

I used to believe that strength meant pretending.
I thought if I could just "man up," "tough it out," "fake it until I made it," somehow the war inside would end.

It didn't.
It got louder.

Real strength isn't hiding your scars. It's refusing to let them stop you.

The truth is, mental health issues don't disappear because you ignore them.
Ignoring them gives them more power.
It took me decades to learn that seeking help is not weakness—it's wisdom.

When the Cracks Show

The cracks showed up everywhere:

In marriages that fell apart after betrayal and heartbreak.

In a lifetime of second-guessing every relationship.

In nights spent staring at ceilings, wondering why I couldn't just be "normal."

At one point, after another marriage ended, I looked at the wreckage around me and finally asked the hardest question:
What if it's not everyone else? What if it's me?

That moment wasn't the end of the battle.
It was the beginning of healing.

The First Step: Admitting the Fight Exists

According to the National Alliance on Mental Illness (NAMI), 1 in 5 adults experience mental illness every year, but less than half receive treatment.

Denial is the first enemy.

And sometimes survival itself can become a kind of denial.

If you're breathing, you're surviving.
But if you're surviving by pretending everything is fine, you're not healing—you're bleeding out slowly.

The first step to changing your life is admitting that you need to.

Your Battle is Not Your Identity

It's easy to believe the lie that because you are broken, you are worthless.
But that's exactly what it is—a lie.

You are not what happened to you.
You are not your diagnosis.
You are not your failures.

You are the fighter who survived all of it.

The American Psychological Association reports that resilience—the ability to adapt after adversity—is one of the strongest predictors of future success.

It's not about never falling.

It's about getting back up, even when you feel like you can't.

Nobody climbs to the top by accident. Every scar is a rung on the ladder.

Today is the First Day

You don't have to solve it all today.
You don't have to be healed to be moving.
You don't have to be fearless to take the first step.

You just have to refuse to quit.

And that's what this book is about—
Refusing to quit.

You are allowed to struggle and still win.
You are allowed to cry and still conquer.
You are allowed to be a mess and still be magnificent.

Mind is the matter.
And this battle is not the end of you—it's the beginning of something greater.

Chapter 2: What They Don't Tell You About Mental Health

The world talks a lot about mental health.

But what they don't talk about is just as important.

They don't tell you how invisible it feels.

They don't tell you how loud the silence can get inside your head.

They don't tell you how many people are quietly fighting the same battles—and losing hope because they think they're alone.

Here's the truth:

Mental Health is Common — and Commonly Misunderstood

According to the Centers for Disease Control and Prevention (CDC):

Over 1 in 5 adults in the United States experience mental illness each year.

1 in 25 adults live with a serious mental illness like bipolar disorder, schizophrenia, or major depression.

Yet despite how common it is, stigma remains strong.

People still say things like "just tough it out" or "it's all in your head," without realizing that the mind is where the battle is.

"Be kind, for everyone you meet is fighting a hard battle."

— Ian Maclaren

The Silent Pressure to Pretend

One of the most damaging myths is the idea that if you were strong enough, you wouldn't need help.

But pretending to be okay doesn't heal you. It isolates you.

The American Psychiatric Association reports that over half of people with mental illness don't seek treatment, mainly due to stigma, fear of judgment, or cultural barriers.

Wearing a mask to get through the day isn't weakness. It's survival. But survival isn't the same thing as healing.

"Healing takes courage, and we all have courage, even if we have to dig a little to find it."

— Tori Amos

It's Not About Willpower

Mental illness isn't a character flaw.

It isn't a lack of faith or willpower.

It's not something you can hustle your way out of.

Brain scans by the National Institute of Mental Health (NIMH) show real biological differences in the brains of people living with depression, PTSD, anxiety, and bipolar disorder.

You wouldn't tell someone with a shattered bone to "walk it off."

You can't tell someone with a wounded mind to just "think positive."

"What mental health needs is more sunlight, more candor, and more unashamed conversation."

— Glenn Close

Race, Culture, and the Stigma Barrier

Mental health stigma doesn't affect everyone equally.

According to the American Psychological Association:

Only 31% of Black adults with mental illness receive treatment.

Only 25% of Asian adults with mental illness seek treatment.

Latino and Native American communities also report major barriers due to stigma, access issues, and cultural beliefs.

In many cultures, seeking therapy is seen as a weakness, or something shameful.

Religious traditions can sometimes offer strength—but can also, at times, reinforce silence by saying prayer alone should "fix it."

**The truth: you can pray
and get professional help.**

You can have faith and use tools to heal.

And no culture, no tradition, and no person should make you feel ashamed for seeking help.

"Faith is taking the first step even when you don't see the whole staircase."

— Martin Luther King Jr.

Trauma Doesn't Expire

Another thing they don't tell you:

Just because something happened a long time ago doesn't mean it's over.

The National Child Traumatic Stress Network reports that untreated childhood trauma often carries into adulthood, affecting relationships, emotional health, physical health, and even success at work.

Time alone doesn't heal trauma.

Healing requires facing it.

"The wound is the place where the Light enters you."

— Rumi

Success Doesn't Mean You're Healed

From the outside, people can seem like they have it all together:

A big job

A beautiful family

A life that looks picture-perfect on social media

But the inside story is often different.

Mental Health America reports that high-functioning depression and anxiety are often overlooked because sufferers appear outwardly successful.

Achievement doesn't cancel out pain.

It just hides it better.

"Success is not final, failure is not fatal: it is the courage to continue that counts."

— Winston Churchill

Healing is Not Linear

Recovery isn't a straight line.

You don't climb up one smooth hill—you fight up a jagged mountain.

The American Psychological Association confirms that relapse and setbacks are normal during mental health recovery.

Falling back into depression, anxiety, or unhealthy patterns doesn't mean you've failed.

It means you are human.

Every fall is a new chance to stand up stronger.

"Our greatest glory is not in never falling, but in rising every time we fall."

— Confucius

What They Won't Tell You: You're Stronger Than You Think

Despite everything you've survived—

Despite trauma, depression, stigma, cultural barriers—

You are still here.

That makes you stronger than you realize.

You don't need to be perfect to be powerful.

You don't need to have it all together to take the next step.

You just have to refuse to give up.

"Strength grows in the moments when you think you can't go on but you keep going anyway."

— Unknown

And if nobody else tells you today:

You're doing better than you think.

Mind is the matter.

And you are stronger than you think.

Chapter 3: Facts That Hit Different

When you hear the phrase "mental health," it's easy to tune it out.

The words are everywhere now—TV, social media, posters in doctor's offices.

But for the people who actually live with it every day, the facts hit different.

Because this isn't a trend. It's reality.

Here's what they don't always tell you:

Mental Health is America's Quiet Epidemic

According to the National Institute of Mental Health (NIMH):

Nearly 1 in 5 adults in the U.S. live with a mental illness.

Anxiety disorders are the most common, affecting over 40 million adults each year.

About 7% of U.S. adults had at least one major depressive episode in the past year.

Yet mental health remains one of the most underfunded, under-treated, and misunderstood health crises.

And the numbers don't lie.

The World Health Organization (WHO) also reports that depression is the leading cause of disability worldwide.

You don't fix the world by pretending it's fine. You fix it by facing what's broken.

**Suicide: The Final Symptom
We Don't Talk About Enough**

The American Foundation for Suicide Prevention reports:

Suicide is the 11th leading cause of death in the United States.

Every year, over 48,000 Americans die by suicide.

There is one death by suicide in the U.S. approximately every 11 minutes.

Among youth and young adults (ages 10–34), suicide is the second leading cause of death.

This isn't just a statistic.

It's a warning.

Mental health struggles are deadly if ignored.

But they are survivable with the right help, the right people, and the right mindset.

"Courage doesn't always roar. Sometimes courage is the quiet voice at the end of the day saying, 'I will try again tomorrow.'"

— Mary Anne Radmacher

Most people have no idea what suicide really looks like.
They think it's a snap decision.
They think it's selfish.
They think it's murder.

They're wrong.

Suicide is a fight.
A brutal, bloody, invisible fight that can last for years.
Every single day, you battle just to stay here.
Every day, you drag yourself through the darkness one more time.

And then one day, you just don't have anything left.

It's not a choice to die.
It's a loss of strength to live.

That's why it makes me furious when some people—especially in churches—use *"Thou shalt not murder"* like a weapon against people who lose that fight.

I've read the Bible front to back, more times than I can count.
You know what I see?
A God who runs toward hurting people, not away from them.
A God who sees the broken and calls them His.
Not a God standing there with a gavel, sending people to hell because they lost a battle no one else could even see.

If you think suicide is just murder, you're not reading the same Bible I am.

When someone takes their own life, it's not because they hated life.
It's because they were too beaten down to keep holding onto it.

And at the moment when families are shattered and grieving—you have the nerve to tell them there's no hope?
No grace?
No mercy?

Trust me.
If that soul had never cried out to God before, they were crying out in those final seconds. They were looking for help anywhere and everywhere!

I know.
Because I've been there.

I've stood at that edge.
I've made the plans, many, many, times.
I've thought about how easy it would be to just stop fighting, because the fight gets so hard!

And the only thing that kept me here was love.

Not lectures.
Not judgment.
Not guilt.
Love.

If you love someone who's struggling, you better understand this:
They don't need your theology lesson.
They need your hand.
They need your heart.

And if you're the one fighting—listen to me:

Find one thing you love.
One reason.
One hope.
Hold on for one more minute.
One more breath.

Because if you can survive this moment, you can survive the next.
And if you survive the next, you'll start to see the light again.

Don't let go.
Not yet.

I've struggled with suicidal thoughts since I was
12 years old. That was the first time I made a
plan to end it. I would have gone through with
it, too—if a girl hadn't come along and
distracted me just enough to put it off.

The truth is, the thoughts never really left.
They lived under the surface for years.

For a long time, my kids were the only thing that
kept me here. I didn't want them growing up
wondering why their father gave up. I stayed
alive for them—because I sure wasn't staying
alive for myself.

But as they grew up and moved out, it got
harder.
The loneliness hit different.
The sense of purpose I used to cling to started
slipping away.
And when they didn't need me the same way
anymore, the darkness came rushing back harder
than ever.

That's when I finally got help.
I started therapy.
I got a service dog.
And even though those years were the darkest
I've ever lived through, they taught me
something I'll never forget:

You need a reason to stay alive.
Because there will be days when *you* aren't enough.
Find that reason—and when everything else falls apart, hang onto it with everything you have.

The Hidden Economic Cost of Mental Illness

Mental health isn't just a personal issue.

It's an economic one.

According to the National Alliance on Mental Illness (NAMI):

Serious mental illness costs America $193.2 billion in lost earnings each year.

Untreated mental health issues cause lower work productivity, higher unemployment, and increased medical expenses.

For individuals, the cost is even more personal—
lost opportunities, lost relationships, lost years
of potential.

Ignoring mental health isn't just dangerous.

It's expensive.

**"If you think education is expensive, try
ignorance."**

— Derek Bok

Getting Help Is Still Hard

Despite all the awareness campaigns, barriers to mental health treatment remain huge:

Cost: Therapy, medication, and hospitalization are expensive, even with insurance.

Availability: In many rural and underserved areas, there are few, if any, qualified mental health professionals.

Stigma: Cultural, racial, and generational beliefs still cause many people to suffer in silence instead of seeking help.

The National Council for Mental Wellbeing found that nearly half of Americans have had to or know someone who has had to travel more than an hour to access mental health care.

The distance between suffering and help isn't just about geography. It's about courage.

Untreated Trauma Doesn't Just Fade Away

The National Child Traumatic Stress Network reports:

About 78% of children reported more than one traumatic experience before the age of 5.

Adults with untreated childhood trauma are at significantly higher risk for depression, anxiety, substance abuse, and suicide.

If trauma isn't processed, it doesn't disappear.

It festers.

Untreated emotional wounds show up everywhere—

In failed relationships.

In addictions.

In physical illnesses.

In self-doubt that never seems to go away.

"The chains of habit are too light to be felt until they are too heavy to be broken."

— Warren Buffett

Why Facts Matter

It's easy to think you're weak if you're struggling.

It's easy to think you should be stronger, faster, better by now.

But facts tell a different story:

Mental health struggles are normal.

Seeking help is brave, not weak.

Healing is possible, but it's rarely linear.

Survival is not failure. It's strength.

"You have been assigned this mountain to show others it can be moved."

— Unknown

You're not failing because you're struggling.

You're winning because you're still standing.

Mind is the matter.

**And every day you fight is another day
you refuse to be defeated.**

Chapter 4: Diagnosis is Not Destiny

When you finally get a diagnosis, it can hit you two ways:

Like a relief, because you finally have a name for what you've been battling.

Or like a life sentence, because you wonder if it will define you forever.

Here's the truth:

A diagnosis explains your struggle.

It doesn't explain your worth.

It doesn't predict your future.

A diagnosis is information. It's not identity.

What a Diagnosis Really Means

According to the National Alliance on Mental Illness (NAMI):

Diagnoses are clinical tools. They describe symptoms, not people.

Diagnoses guide treatment, not fate. They are meant to help doctors create a plan, not to box you in.

Diagnoses can change. Many people are misdiagnosed early in their mental health journey.

The American Psychiatric Association acknowledges that mental health diagnoses are often based on patterns of behavior, not simple blood tests or x-rays.

That means they are the beginning of
understanding—not the final word on your life.

You are more than a chart.

You are more than a label.

You are a human being, not a case file.

"Labels are for cans, not for people."

— Anthony Rapp

Some of the Greatest Minds in History Battled
Mental Illness

A diagnosis doesn't mean you're doomed.

In fact, many of history's most brilliant,
successful people lived with mental health
struggles:

Abraham Lincoln — Battled depression
throughout his life.

Winston Churchill — Called his depression "the black dog" but still led Britain through its darkest hours.

Princess Diana — Publicly shared her battle with depression and bulimia.

Demi Lovato — Lives openly with bipolar disorder while maintaining a powerful career.

Ernest Hemingway — Struggled with bipolar disorder and depression while becoming one of the most influential writers in history.

These names aren't remembered for their diagnoses.

They're remembered for their impact.

"Success is not final, failure is not fatal: it is the courage to continue that counts."

— Winston Churchill

You Are Not Broken Beyond Repair

When you live with a mental health condition, it's easy to believe you're damaged goods.

But that belief is a lie.

Psychology Today reports that with proper treatment, the vast majority of people living with mental illness see significant improvement in symptoms and quality of life.

Treatment can mean different things:

Therapy

Medication

Lifestyle changes

Faith and community support

New coping strategies

It's not about curing yourself overnight.

It's about building a life where healing is part of the journey—not a finish line.

"Healing doesn't mean the damage never existed. It means the damage no longer controls your life."

— Akshay Dubey

The Power of Ownership

One of the biggest shifts in your mental health journey is this:

You can't always control what happens to you.

You can control how you respond to it.

Taking ownership doesn't mean you caused your illness.

It means you choose what happens next.

"You don't control the storm, but you can control your sail."

Eric F. Gilbert, From Broke to Business Boss

Ownership is power.

It shifts you from victim to victor.

You are not the story written about you.

You are the author now.

Healing is Messy — and Worth It

No one hands you a neat little recovery timeline.

Healing looks different for everyone.

Some days you'll make progress.

Some days it will feel like you're moving backward.

That doesn't mean you're losing.

It means you're fighting.

The American Psychological Association confirms that mental health recovery is non-linear, often involving setbacks, breakthroughs, and rebuilding.

"Fall seven times, stand up eight."

— Japanese Proverb

Diagnosis is Information, Not Identity

Here's what the facts say:

Diagnosis is a starting point, not an ending.

Treatment works, and people recover.

You are not your diagnosis.

The mind is powerful.
It can break you down—but it can also rebuild you stronger than before.

Diagnosis doesn't define you.
Your decisions do.

Mind is the matter.

And you are bigger than anything
you've been labeled.

Chapter 5: You Can Still Win

Mental health struggles can feel like a thief—stealing time, stealing energy, stealing hope.

But the truth is this: you can still win.

Not in spite of your struggle, but because you fought through it.

Your story isn't over. It's just getting started.

Winning Doesn't Mean the Absence of Struggle

According to the National Alliance on Mental Illness (NAMI):

1 in 5 adults in the U.S. experience mental illness each year.

Many of those people still finish school, start businesses, build families, and lead meaningful lives.

The media often paints a picture where success means perfect mental health, but reality tells a different story.

You can succeed while managing anxiety.

You can grow while battling depression.

You can win even when the fight never fully goes away.

"Victory is not winning every battle. Victory is refusing to surrender."

Eric F. Gilbert, From Broke to Business Boss

Your Struggles Can Shape Your Strengths

Psychologists have found that people who overcome mental health challenges often develop:

Greater resilience

Higher emotional intelligence

Stronger empathy for others

Increased creativity

The American Psychological Association states that post-traumatic growth is real: people often experience positive psychological change as a result of struggling with highly challenging life circumstances.

Your scars are not signs of weakness.

They are signs of survival.

"Out of suffering have emerged the strongest souls; the most massive characters are seared with scars."

— Khalil Gibran

It's Not How Fast You Go. It's That You Don't Stop.

Social media loves overnight success stories.

But real success often looks like this:

Fighting your way through depression just to show up today.

Taking medication and getting to therapy even when you don't want to.

Building your business, your family, your life,
even when your mind tells you that you can't.

Success isn't about speed.

It's about endurance.

"Most people overestimate what they can do
in one year and underestimate what they can
do in ten years."

— Bill Gates

Small steps add up.

Daily decisions stack into victories over time.

Your Mind Will Lie to You. Facts Won't.

When you're in a low place, your mind will tell
you:

"You're broken."

"You're behind."

"You're not good enough."

"You'll never make it."

But the facts say otherwise.

The National Institute of Mental Health reports
that with treatment, 70–90% of individuals have
a significant reduction of symptoms and
improved quality of life.

You can get better.

You can heal.

You can win—even if your mind tells you
otherwise.

"Don't believe everything you think."

— Unknown

Your Success Might Look Different — and That's Okay

Winning might not look like a mansion or a trophy.

It might look like:

A healthy relationship after years of toxic ones.

Starting your own business even when you doubted you could.

Waking up one more day and deciding not to quit.

Victory is personal.

Victory is progress.

Victory is deciding to keep building, no matter how slow it feels.

"Success is liking yourself, liking what you do, and liking how you do it."

— Maya Angelou

You Can Still Win — And You Will

If you're breathing, you're still in the game.

If you're trying, you're still in the fight.

And if you're still fighting, you can still win.

Your past didn't disqualify you.

Your diagnosis didn't eliminate you.

Your scars didn't erase your future.

Mind is the matter.

And you were made to overcome.

Chapter 6: Mind Hacks for the Dark Days

Everyone has dark days.

But when you live with mental health challenges, dark days can feel heavier, louder, and harder to escape.

The goal isn't to pretend they don't exist.

The goal is to have tools that help you survive them.

Here are proven, fact-based strategies—mind hacks—to help you make it through when it feels impossible.

1. Move Your Body

According to Harvard Medical School:

Exercise can be as effective as antidepressant medication for some people.

Physical activity releases endorphins—your brain's natural mood boosters.

You don't have to run a marathon.

A 10-minute walk

Stretching

Yoga

Lifting light weights

Movement reminds your mind that you're still in control.

"It does not matter how slowly you go as long as you do not stop."

— Confucius

2. Reframe Your Thinking

Negative thoughts are like weeds—they grow fast and choke out the good.

Cognitive Behavioral Therapy (CBT), one of the most researched mental health treatments, is based on challenging and reframing negative thoughts.

Examples:

From "I'll never get better" → to → "Healing takes time, but I'm working on it."

From "I'm worthless" → to → "My worth is not defined by today's feelings."

"Whether you think you can, or you think you can't—you're right."

— Henry Ford

3. Build a Crisis Plan Before You Need It

On your best days, build a plan for your worst days.

Mental Health America suggests creating a Personal Crisis Plan including:

Emergency contacts

Safe activities (music, walking, journaling)

Reasons to keep going

Coping strategies that have worked before

When your mind is loud, your plan can think for you.

"You don't rise to the level of your goals. You fall to the level of your systems."

— James Clear, Atomic Habits

4. Break the Day Into Tiny Pieces

When the day feels too big, shrink it.

Psychology Today recommends using micro-goals on overwhelming days:

"I will make my bed."

"I will shower."

"I will eat one meal."

"I will walk outside for two minutes."

Micro-goals create momentum, and momentum creates hope.

"Small deeds done are better than great deeds planned."

— Peter Marshall

5. Connect—Even If You Don't Feel Like It

Isolation feeds darkness.

It tells you nobody cares.

It tells you you're better off alone.

But research by the American Psychological Association shows that social support is a major protective factor against depression and suicide.

Checking in with friends can be vital.

Even when all you want is to hide, reaching out can save your life.

A simple message like, "Thinking about you—how's everything going?" can break the silence.

Solitude might feel safer during depression—but it's actually your enemy.

According to the CDC, people who feel socially isolated are nearly twice as likely to experience depression, anxiety, and suicidal thoughts compared to those with regular social interaction.

"We are all broken, that's how the light gets in."

— Ernest Hemingway

6. Alcohol is Not Your Friend

When you're struggling, alcohol can seem like the easiest escape.

But it is a trap.

The National Institute on Alcohol Abuse and Alcoholism (NIAAA) reports that:

About 30% of people with major depression also struggle with alcohol abuse.

Alcohol is a depressant, meaning it worsens symptoms of sadness, hopelessness, and anxiety over time.

What feels like temporary relief quickly turns into deeper darkness.

Alcohol numbs pain for a moment—and then magnifies it.

"You can't drown your demons. They know how to swim."

— Unknown

7. Service Animals: Unexpected Lifesavers

During my darkest times, I was able to get a service dog.

And without exaggeration, he kept me alive.

There were months so dark that I could not leave the house without him.

He was magic.

There were many days where the only reason I got out of bed was because he needed to go outside.

If it wasn't for him, I literally wouldn't be here today.

He was trained to alert me when I needed to take anxiety meds (I have anxiety related high blood pressure, which ahs landed me in the ER several times).

I suffer from chronic pain and migraines, and he seemed to know when I was in pain. Only when I was in pain would he lay next to me to comfort me. The rest of the time he stayed close.

Service animals are not a gimmick—they are a lifeline.

The National Institutes of Health (NIH) reports that service dogs can significantly reduce PTSD symptoms, depression, and anxiety among people battling severe mental health challenges.

If you're in a place where you're struggling to care for yourself, looking into getting a service dog could be life-changing.

They don't just walk with you.

They pull you back from the edge.

8. Remind Yourself: Feelings Are Not Facts

Feelings are real.

But they are not always true.

When you're deep in depression, your mind whispers lies:

"Nobody loves you."

"You're a burden."

"It will never get better."

The truth is, emotions are temporary chemical storms in the brain.

You don't have to believe every thought you have.

"The darkest hour has only sixty minutes."

— Morris Mandel

9. Protect Your Sleep Like Your Life Depends on It

Because it does.

Johns Hopkins Medicine reports that sleep problems are both a symptom and a cause of worsening mental health.

Lack of sleep increases the risk of depression, anxiety, and even suicidal thoughts.

Protect your sleep by:

Keeping a regular bedtime

Turning off screens an hour before bed

Limiting caffeine and alcohol late in the day.

You might think that alcohol helps you sleep,
but while it might help you fall asleep, it does far
more damage to your night's sleep than good.

Alcohol is NOT your friend!

Creating a calm, dark sleeping environment

Sleep isn't a luxury.

It's survival.

**"A good laugh and a long sleep are the two
best cures for anything."**

— Irish Proverb

The Truth About Dark Days

You can't always stop dark days from coming.

But you can survive them.

And survival is success.

You don't have to be perfect.

You don't have to be fearless.

You just have to keep breathing, keep moving, and keep believing that the dark day is not the last day.

Mind is the matter.

And the darkness never gets to win unless you stop walking toward the light.

Chapter 7: Rebuilding Confidence After It's Been Shattered

When mental illness, trauma, or failure knocks you down, it doesn't just bruise your mind—it wrecks your confidence.

Confidence isn't about arrogance.

Confidence is the belief that you have the ability to survive, to grow, to succeed.

When you lose that, it feels like you lose yourself.

The good news is this:

Confidence can be rebuilt.

Stronger. Wiser. Fiercer than before.

How Mental Health Battles Break Confidence

According to the American Psychological Association:

Low self-esteem is a frequent companion of depression, anxiety, PTSD, and other mental health conditions.

Trauma survivors often internalize guilt, shame, and helplessness.

When your brain tells you you're broken for long enough, you start to believe it.

The first step to rebuilding confidence is knowing that it's not your fault.

The second step is deciding that it's not permanent.

"You may have to fight a battle more than once to win it."

— Margaret Thatcher

Step 1: Name the Lies

Your mind lies when it's sick.

It tells you:

"You are worthless."

"You always fail."

"Nobody would miss you."

These thoughts are symptoms—not reality.

Cognitive Behavioral Therapy research shows that challenging and reframing distorted thoughts leads to real improvements in mood and self-confidence.

Catch the lie.

Call it out.

Replace it with truth.

"Believe you can and you're halfway there."

— Theodore Roosevelt

Step 2: Stack Small Wins

Confidence doesn't return all at once.

It comes back through small victories, day by day.

Psychology Today emphasizes that achieving small, manageable goals reactivates the brain's reward center, helping rebuild self-belief.

Examples:

Finishing a project

Reaching out to a friend

Exercising for 10 minutes

Showing up on a hard day

Each win reminds you:

You are capable.

You are not powerless.

"Success is the sum of small efforts, repeated day in and day out."

— Robert Collier

Step 3: Remove the Voices That Tear You Down

Not everyone deserves a front-row seat in your life.

Toxic relationships can suffocate whatever confidence you're trying to rebuild.

Research from the Mayo Clinic shows that supportive social environments improve mental health recovery rates dramatically, while toxic ones delay healing.

If someone:

Belittles your progress

Doubts your ability to heal

Triggers your worst feelings

It's time to create distance.

You're allowed to outgrow people who refuse to grow with you.

"You are the average of the five people you spend the most time with."

— Jim Rohn

Step 4: Celebrate Progress, Not Perfection

Healing and rebuilding aren't linear.

Some days you'll feel strong.

Some days you'll feel broken again.

That's normal.

That's human.

The key is to celebrate progress, not perfection.

The American Psychological Association states that self-compassion improves resilience, reduces anxiety, and strengthens confidence.

Beating yourself up doesn't rebuild you.

Cheering yourself on does.

> **"It's not whether you get knocked down, it's whether you get up."**
>
> **— Vince Lombardi**

Step 5: Reconnect with Your Strengths

Your illness didn't erase your strengths.

Your trauma didn't erase your talents.

They're still there, waiting for you to pick them up again.

Research from Positive Psychology studies shows that focusing on your existing strengths increases happiness, engagement, and confidence.

Maybe you're:

A good listener

A creative thinker

A hard worker

A loyal friend

Whatever it is—reclaim it.

Strength isn't pretending you were never hurt.
Strength is standing up even when you were.

**"Strength doesn't come from what you can
do. It comes from overcoming the things you
once thought you couldn't."**

— Rikki Rogers

Confidence Isn't Lost Forever

It's shattered, not destroyed.

It's buried, not erased.

It's bruised, not broken beyond repair.

Confidence is rebuilt every time you refuse to believe that the worst thing that happened to you is the last word on your life.

Mind is the matter.

And you are more powerful than you remember.

Chapter 8: Relationships and Mental Health

Relationships can be the greatest source of strength—or the greatest trigger of struggle—when you're living with mental health challenges.

Loving others and allowing yourself to be loved can feel overwhelming when your own mind feels unstable.

But relationships are vital to survival, healing, and growth.

Why Mental Illness Affects Relationships

The National Alliance on Mental Illness (NAMI) reports:

Nearly two-thirds of people with mental health conditions say their relationships have been negatively impacted.

Common struggles include communication issues, emotional withdrawal, irritability, trust issues, and feelings of guilt or burden.

Mental illness affects how you see yourself—and how you see others.

Depression tells you you're unworthy of love.

Anxiety tells you people will leave.

Trauma teaches you to expect betrayal.

Recognizing this pattern is the first step toward changing it.

"The greatest thing you'll ever learn is just to love and be loved in return."

— Eden Ahbez

Communication is Survival

The American Psychological Association emphasizes that open, honest communication is critical in maintaining healthy relationships during mental health struggles.

When you don't talk about what you're feeling, people fill in the blanks—and usually not correctly.

Practical steps:

Tell trusted people when you're struggling.

Be honest about what you need (space, support, help).

Explain that bad days don't mean you don't care.

You don't have to tell everyone everything.

But silence leaves too much room for misunderstanding.

"Clear is kind. Unclear is unkind."

— Brené Brown

Boundaries Protect Both Sides

Boundaries are not walls.

They are fences with gates—allowing in the right people, keeping out what harms you.

According to the Mayo Clinic:

Setting healthy boundaries reduces stress, prevents resentment, and strengthens trust.

Boundaries might mean:

Saying "no" without guilt.

Protecting your healing time.

Choosing not to engage in toxic arguments.

Asking for space when you need it.

Boundaries protect both your mental health and your relationships.

"Daring to set boundaries is about having the courage to love ourselves, even when we risk disappointing others."

— Brené Brown

Choosing the Right People

Not everyone will understand your struggle.

Not everyone deserves access to your heart.

Research shows that people with strong, supportive social networks have better mental health outcomes and lower relapse rates (American Psychological Association).

Healthy people:

Listen without judgment.

Offer help without controlling you.

Encourage your healing without rushing you.

Toxic people:

Dismiss your experiences.

Make you feel guilty for needing help.

Drain your energy instead of filling it.

You are allowed to choose your tribe carefully.

"Surround yourself only with people who are going to lift you higher."

— Oprah Winfrey

Self-Love Makes Every Relationship Stronger

It's nearly impossible to accept love fully from others if you don't believe you deserve it yourself.

According to Positive Psychology research:

Self-compassion leads to more satisfying and resilient relationships.

Healing your relationship with yourself improves every other relationship in your life.

Self-love isn't arrogance.

Self-love is survival.

Here's the truth:

You are special.

You are important.

You have a purpose that only you can fulfill.

Even though you might see flaws when you look in the mirror, others see beauty.

Not everyone is attracted to the "perfect" media version of beauty.

Everyone likes something different.

Someone out there thinks you are exactly what they've been hoping for.

The world sells you a lie about perfection:

Flawless skin

Perfect body

Perfect smile

Perfect success

But real life doesn't work that way.

Real life is messy, human, beautiful in all its diversity.

Stop measuring yourself against a fake standard.

You are already worthy.

You are already valuable.

You are already enough.

Ways to practice self-love:

Speak to yourself kindly.

Forgive yourself for past mistakes.

Treat yourself with the patience you give others.

Celebrate the parts of you that make you different, not ashamed.

"You yourself, as much as anybody in the entire universe, deserve your love and affection."

— Buddha

When You Love Someone with Mental Illness

Sometimes you're on the other side—loving someone who struggles.

Here's what experts recommend:

Educate yourself about their condition.

Listen more than you advise.

Don't take mood swings personally.

Encourage professional help without trying to be their therapist.

Take care of your own mental health too.

Loving someone through their battle is hard.

But real love doesn't leave when the war starts.

"Love is not a victory march. It's a cold and it's a broken hallelujah."

— Leonard Cohen

Relationships Are Hard — But Worth It

Relationships require patience, forgiveness, communication, and courage—especially when mental health challenges are part of the story.

But they are worth it.

Real connection is worth fighting for.

Love is worth fighting for.

Mind is the matter.

**And you are worth loving
broken, healing, messy, real.**

Chapter 9: Turning Pain Into Power

Pain changes people.

It either breaks them—or it builds them.

The truth is, pain is a powerful force.

It can leave you bitter, broken, and stuck.

Or it can forge you into something stronger, wiser, and unstoppable.

Pain is inevitable.

What you do with it is optional.

Pain is a Universal Experience

According to the American Psychological Association:

Everyone experiences emotional pain.

Trauma, loss, betrayal, and disappointment are part of the human condition.

Pain isn't a punishment.

It's part of living.

You are not weak because you hurt.

You are human because you hurt.

"Out of suffering have emerged the strongest souls; the most massive characters are seared with scars."

— Khalil Gibran

We're All Hiding Pain

Here's something most people won't tell you:

Everyone you meet is struggling with something.

This is not to shrug off your pain or minimize what you're going through.

Your pain is real. It matters.

But it's also important to understand that you are not alone in this fight.

Most of the people around you—the ones who look like they have it all together—are carrying hidden battles, too.

Behind the smiles, behind the success, behind the masks, there is pain.

We are all hurting in some way.

We are all pushing through something.

Don't give up because you think you're the only broken one.

You're not broken beyond repair—you're human.

Keep pushing through the pain.

You're not alone.

You're not the only one struggling.

And you're not the only one who will survive.

"Be kind, for everyone you meet is fighting a hard battle."

— Ian Maclaren

The Science of Post-Traumatic Growth

While trauma can cause deep wounds, it can also trigger Post-Traumatic Growth (PTG).

The concept, first identified by psychologists Richard Tedeschi and Lawrence Calhoun, shows that:

Many people experience positive psychological changes after trauma.

Growth often occurs in areas like relationships, personal strength, appreciation of life, spiritual development, and new possibilities.

Surviving doesn't just make you tougher.

It can make you deeper.

It can make you better.

"The world breaks everyone, and afterward, many are strong at the broken places."

Your Story Can Be Someone Else's Survival Guide

Your pain has the power to help others.

When you share what you've been through, you shine a light for someone still stuck in the dark.

According to research published in the Journal of Positive Psychology:

Helping others after personal adversity is linked to greater self-esteem, happiness, and mental health resilience.

You don't have to be healed to be helpful.

You just have to be honest.

> "Your greatest test is your greatest testimony."
>
> — Unknown

Using Pain as Fuel, Not a Chain

Pain can trap you.

Or pain can drive you.

The choice is whether you let it define you—or refine you.

Psychology Today reports that setting meaningful goals after trauma often transforms suffering into a sense of purpose, improving mental health outcomes.

Use your experiences to:

Fuel your ambition

Fuel your compassion

Fuel your drive to make a difference

Your scars can be your fuel, not your chains.

"Turn your wounds into wisdom."

— Oprah Winfrey

Purpose Can Rise From Pain

Pain makes you ask bigger questions:

Why am I here?

What am I supposed to do with what I've lived through?

How can I make this matter?

Finding purpose doesn't erase the pain.

It gives the pain meaning.

According to the Greater Good Science Center at UC Berkeley:

Having a sense of purpose dramatically improves resilience, health, and life satisfaction, even among trauma survivors.

You were not born just to suffer.

You were born to overcome—and to leave a mark that only you can leave.

"He who has a why to live for can bear almost any how."

— Friedrich Nietzsche

Your Pain is Not the End of Your Story

Pain changes you.

But it doesn't have to end you.

You are still breathing.

You are still becoming.

You are still building something no one else can build.

Mind is the matter.

And your pain is just the
beginning of your power.

Chapter 10: The Comeback Is Always Bigger Than the Setback

Setbacks are part of life.

Especially when you're battling mental health challenges, it can feel like two steps forward, ten steps back.

But the real truth is this:

Every setback you survive sets you up for a bigger comeback.

It doesn't matter how far you fall.

It matters that you get up.

Setbacks Are Normal

According to the American Psychological Association:

Relapses in depression, anxiety, PTSD, and bipolar disorder are common, even during treatment.

Setbacks are not signs of failure—they are part of the recovery process.

You are not doing it wrong because you fall down sometimes.

You are doing it right because you refuse to stay down.

"Our greatest glory is not in never falling, but in rising every time we fall."

— Confucius

Comebacks Are Built in the Dark

Most people think a comeback is about having a big moment where everything suddenly gets better.

But real comebacks are built in silence, in pain, in persistence.

Research from the Journal of Behavioral Medicine shows that perseverance and resilience after trauma are major predictors of future life satisfaction.

Nobody sees the lonely nights, the slow progress, the hundreds of small battles you win in private.

But those are the battles that matter most.

"It's not whether you get knocked down, it's whether you get up."

— Vince Lombardi

Every Setback Teaches You Something

Pain teaches you what comfort cannot.

Failure teaches you what success hides.

Setbacks strip away what's fake and leave behind what's real.

Psychologists call this adversarial growth:

The process of becoming stronger, wiser, and more focused because of hardship.

Every time you rise, you know yourself better.

You know your strength better.

You know your worth better.

"Difficulties in life are intended to make us better, not bitter."

— Dan Reeves

Mindset Turns Setbacks Into Fuel

You can't always control what happens.

But you can control what you make it mean.

The Mayo Clinic notes that optimistic thinking is linked to faster recovery from depression and anxiety, better heart health, and longer lifespan.

It's not about pretending everything is fine.

It's about believing that even the bad things can lead somewhere good if you refuse to quit.

Mindset doesn't remove the obstacles.

It builds the engine that drives through them.

"The only limit to our realization of tomorrow is our doubts of today."

— Franklin D. Roosevelt

Real-Life Comebacks That Inspire

History is filled with people who turned devastating setbacks into unbelievable comebacks:

Oprah Winfrey — Fired from her first television job and told she was "unfit for TV."

Michael Jordan — Cut from his high school basketball team.

J.K. Rowling — Rejected by dozens of publishers before Harry Potter became a global phenomenon.

Abraham Lincoln — Lost multiple elections and suffered personal tragedies before becoming one of the greatest U.S. Presidents.

None of them won because life was easy.

They won because they refused to let defeat define them.

"Success is not final, failure is not fatal: it is the courage to continue that counts."

— Winston Churchill

Your Comeback Will Be Bigger Than Your Setback

The size of your comeback isn't measured by how low you fell.

It's measured by how high you rise back up.

Your mental health struggles, your losses, your dark days—they do not disqualify you.

They prepare you.

Mind is the matter.

And the only thing more powerful than a setback is the fighter who gets back up after it.

You're still standing.

You're still building.

And your comeback story isn't finished yet.

Chapter 11: Forged in the Fire: How Struggle Becomes Strength

The world teaches us to hide our struggles.

But the truth is:

The very thing you thought would destroy you may be the thing that gives you your greatest strength.

Your battle doesn't make you less.

It makes you more.

And the battlefield where your victory begins—or ends—is your mind.

Struggle Builds Strength

According to the American Psychological Association:

Resilience is developed, not inherited.

People who experience hardship and overcome it often have higher resilience, better problem-solving skills, and stronger emotional intelligence.

The pain you survive sharpens you in ways comfort never could.

You don't build muscle without resistance.

You don't build character without challenge.

"Strength does not come from physical capacity. It comes from an indomitable will."

— Mahatma Gandhi

Vulnerability is Power

Society trains us to hide our broken places.

But vulnerability isn't weakness—it's a weapon.

Research by Dr. Brené Brown shows:

Vulnerability increases courage, emotional connection, and real leadership ability.

When you have the courage to be real about your struggle, you inspire others to be real too.

And real connection is what changes lives.

"Vulnerability sounds like truth and feels like courage. Truth and courage aren't always comfortable, but they're never weakness."

— Brené Brown

Pain Sharpens Your Purpose

According to the Greater Good Science Center:

Survivors of adversity often experience greater clarity about life purpose and priorities.

When you've been broken and survived it:

You value time differently.

You value people differently.

You see opportunities where others only see obstacles.

Your pain becomes your purpose.

Your scars become your map.

> **"The wound is the place where the Light enters you."**
>
> **— Rumi**

Empathy Is Forged in Fire

You can't fake true empathy.

It comes from walking through the fire yourself.

Studies show that:

Experiencing pain often leads to greater empathy and compassion for others.

You understand hurt differently when you've lived it.

You notice suffering in others because you carry your own memories of it.

Empathy becomes your superpower.

Not because you read about struggle—but because you survived it.

 "Be kind. Everyone you meet is fighting a battle you know nothing about."

— Ian Maclaren

Creativity Is Born from Struggle

Pain doesn't just break things.

It builds things.

Research in Frontiers in Psychology shows:

Adversity fuels creativity and innovation by forcing new ways of thinking.

The same mind that battled darkness can create light.

The same soul that endured suffering can give life to new ideas, new art, and new hope.

"Art is born of humiliation."

— W.H. Auden

Your Mind Is the Battlefield

The greatest fight of your life isn't outside you.

It's inside you.

According to the National Institute of Mental Health:

Our thoughts directly influence our emotions, behaviors, and overall mental health.

If you lose the battle in your mind, you lose everywhere else.

But if you win it—you can survive anything.

Every day you have to fight:

Lies that say you're not enough

Doubts that say you can't make it

Fears that say it's not worth trying

The fight is real.

The mind is the matter.

"As a man thinketh in his heart, so is he."

— Proverbs 23:7

Thoughts Become Weapons

Psychology Today reports:

Negative thinking patterns increase risk for depression, anxiety, and even physical health problems.

Positive, realistic thinking improves resilience, recovery rates, and life satisfaction.

Your thoughts are either fighting for you—or against you.

Mastering your mind doesn't mean lying to yourself.

It means telling yourself the truth louder than the lies.

Truth like:

"I am worthy of healing."

"I am allowed to struggle and still win."

"I am stronger than the worst thing that ever happened to me."

"Whether you think you can or you think you can't, you're right."

— Henry Ford

You Are Already Winning

You are fighting battles most people never see.

You have survived days most people couldn't imagine.

Every time you refuse to give up, you win.

Every time you choose to believe in hope one more day, you win.

Mind is the matter.

**And you are more
powerful than you know.**

Chapter 12: Mental Health and Success Are Not Opposites

Society sends a dangerous message:

If you struggle with mental health, you can't be successful.

That is a lie.

Mental health challenges don't disqualify you from winning in life.

In fact, many of the most successful people in history carried invisible battles behind their achievements.

You don't have to choose between survival and success.

You can have both.

The Reality Behind the Spotlight

According to the National Alliance on Mental Illness (NAMI):

Nearly 1 in 5 adults live with mental health conditions, including CEOs, athletes, celebrities, and leaders.

Mental health issues are not rare among high achievers.

They are common.

Examples:

Simone Biles, Olympic gold medalist, openly discusses her struggles with anxiety and trauma.

Dwayne "The Rock" Johnson has spoken publicly about battling depression.

Lady Gaga has been vocal about her PTSD and chronic mental health struggles.

Elon Musk has discussed his experience with bipolar symptoms.

Success and struggle often live side by side.

"The strongest people are not those who show strength in front of us, but those who win battles we know nothing about."

— Unknown

Struggle Can Sharpen Skills

Psychological research shows that:

Facing and managing mental health struggles often strengthens leadership, resilience, creativity, empathy, and problem-solving skills.

These are the very traits that fuel long-term success.

Your challenges don't subtract from your ability to succeed.

They add depth, toughness, and perspective.

"Success is going from failure to failure without losing your enthusiasm."

— Winston Churchill

Mental Health Management Is a Success Strategy

Managing your mental health is managing your future.

The American Psychological Association emphasizes that:

Self-care practices, therapy, medication when necessary, and stress management are not weaknesses—they are strategic strengths.

Taking care of your mind is just as critical as taking care of your body or your business.

Smart, successful people know when to rest.

They know when to ask for help.

They know survival is a skill.

"Rest when you're weary. Refresh and renew yourself, your body, your mind, your spirit. Then get back to work."

— Ralph Marston

Resilience is the Hidden Advantage

People who have fought for their peace every day know something others don't:

How to keep moving under pressure.

How to rebuild after losing everything.

How to lead with empathy because they know what pain feels like.

According to Harvard Business Review, resilience is one of the top predictors of executive success and effective leadership.

You're not "less than" because you struggle.

You're "more than" because you survived.

"Hardships often prepare ordinary people for an extraordinary destiny."

— C.S. Lewis

Your Struggle Is Part of Your Story—Not the End

Your mental health battles are chapters in your story.

They are not the conclusion.

You can build companies.

You can lead teams.

You can inspire nations.

You can change lives.

You can succeed not because you were untouched by struggle—but because you refused to be defined by it.

Mind is the matter.

And your future is still being written by your courage, your persistence, and your refusal to quit.

Chapter 13: Mental Health Survival Tools:
The Everyday Weapons You Need

Motivation is powerful.

But on the worst days, motivation alone isn't enough.

You need weapons for the battle happening inside your mind.

This chapter isn't theory.

It's real, tactical tools—backed by science, tested in real life—to help you survive, recover, and keep building the life you deserve.

1. Build Your Mental First Aid Kit

Just like a physical injury needs a first aid kit, your mind needs one too.

According to the Mental Health First Aid organization:

Having a pre-built action plan reduces the intensity and duration of mental health crises.

Your Mental First Aid Kit should include:

A list of 3 people you can call or text

A list of small activities that bring you comfort (walking, music, prayer, journaling)

Grounding techniques you know work for you

Crisis hotline numbers saved in your phone

A simple written reminder: "This feeling will pass."

You don't want to build your plan during a storm.

You want it ready before the storm hits.

"By failing to prepare, you are preparing to fail."

— Benjamin Franklin

2. Create a "Low Day" Plan

When you are in a dark place, decision-making becomes harder.

A "Low Day" Plan makes survival automatic.

According to the American Psychological Association:

Pre-planning coping strategies significantly improves emotional recovery during mental health episodes.

Your Low Day Plan should be simple, realistic, and non-negotiable:

Take your meds.

Eat at least one real meal.

Walk outside for 5 minutes.

Text someone you trust.

Write down 3 reasons you're still fighting.

You don't have to thrive on the worst days.
You just have to survive.

3. Use Grounding Techniques

Grounding techniques pull you back into the present when anxiety, trauma flashbacks, or depression try to drag you under.

Science-backed grounding exercises include:

5-4-3-2-1 Method:

5 things you can see

4 things you can feel

3 things you can hear

2 things you can smell

1 thing you can taste

Deep Breathing:

Inhale for 4 seconds

Hold for 4 seconds

Exhale for 6 seconds

(reduces cortisol, the body's stress hormone)

Grounding gives your mind something stronger to hold onto than fear or despair.

"Feelings are much like waves: we can't stop them from coming, but we can choose which ones to surf."

— Jonatan Mårtensson

4. Create Your Mental Safe Place

Another tool that has proven incredibly powerful is visualization of a safe place.

My therapist once asked me to imagine a place where I felt completely at peace, totally in control, and fully safe.

For me, that place was early mornings on my kayak—

Gliding through quiet water, no phone calls, no noise, knowing the waters around me like the back of my hand.

Just thinking about that place calmed my body and mind almost instantly.

I took a photo the next time I was out there and made it my phone background—

So now, anytime I need to, I can look at that photo and be transported back into that feeling of peace.

This is a proven grounding and visualization technique, supported by mental health professionals:

Visualizing a safe place helps regulate the nervous system, reduce panic symptoms, and restore emotional control.

To create your own:

Close your eyes and think of a place where you feel calm, strong, and safe.

Picture it with all your senses—what you see, hear, smell, and feel.

Keep a physical reminder (photo, background, note) where you can access it during tough moments.

You can carry peace with you—even into the darkest days.

5. Set Micro-Goals

When you're overwhelmed, big goals feel impossible.

Research from Psychology Today confirms:

Micro-goals (small, achievable actions) create momentum and positive feedback loops for mental health recovery.

Examples of micro-goals:

Brush your teeth

Reply to one email

Make your bed

Step outside and breathe fresh air

Victory isn't about speed.

It's about direction.

6. Identify Your Anchor People

Isolation is dangerous during mental health battles.

According to the CDC:

Social connectedness is one of the strongest predictors of resilience and suicide prevention.

Your "Anchor People" are the few who:

Don't judge you for struggling

Listen without trying to fix everything

Remind you who you are when you forget

If you don't have anchor people yet, it's worth building those connections now—even if it's just one person.

"Sometimes carrying someone else's light for a while saves their life."

— Unknown

7. Journal the Fight

Writing out your thoughts gets them out of your head and onto paper.

Research from Cambridge University shows:

Expressive writing improves mental and emotional recovery after trauma and stress.

You don't need perfect grammar or deep insights.

You just need honesty.

Write about:

What you're feeling

What triggered it

What you're doing to survive today

The page can carry what your mind can't.

8. Respect the Reset

Sometimes the strongest thing you can do is reset instead of pushing harder.

The Mayo Clinic highlights that:

Rest and recovery are essential to mental health management.

Reset doesn't mean quit.
Reset means recharge.

A reset might look like:

Turning off your phone for a day

Sleeping without guilt

Saying "no" to unnecessary obligations

Taking a mental health day unapologetically

Rest is not a reward.

It's a requirement.

9. Monitor Your Inner Dialogue

Your brain believes what you tell it most often.

According to the National Institutes of Health:

Self-talk patterns strongly influence depression, anxiety, recovery rates, and long-term resilience.

Check what you're saying to yourself:

Replace "I'm a failure" with "I'm fighting harder than most."

Replace "I'll never get better" with "Healing isn't linear, and that's okay."

Replace "Nobody cares" with "Some people care—and I need to let them."

You are either building yourself or breaking yourself with your words.

"The mind is everything. What you think, you become."

— Buddha

10. Recognize Progress (Even When It's Invisible)

Not all progress looks dramatic.

Sometimes survival is progress.

Every time you:

Get up when you didn't want to

Stay alive through one more dark day

Choose recovery over giving up

You are winning battles nobody sees.

According to Positive Psychology studies:

Recognizing small wins builds the brain's resilience pathways, making future battles easier to survive.

Celebrate quietly if you have to.

But celebrate.

You're moving forward—even if it's just one inch
today.

Final Word on Tools

Mental health battles aren't fought by "waiting to feel better."

They're fought by arming yourself daily with the tools that work.

You're not weak because you need strategies.

You're smart because you use them.

Mind is the matter.

And when you fight with the right weapons you win more than you lose.

Chapter 14: Daily Mental Health Routine: Winning the Fight One Day at a Time

Big battles are won by small disciplines.

When it comes to managing your mental health, there is no magic fix.

There are only daily actions that build strength, resilience, and hope over time.

According to research from the American Psychological Association:

Daily routines reduce anxiety, lower depression symptoms, and improve recovery outcomes in people facing mental health challenges.

This isn't about perfection.

This is about survival strategies that become survival habits.

Here's how to build your daily mental health armor.

1. Morning Mental Armor

The first 15 minutes after you wake up set the tone for your entire day.

Studies from Harvard Medical School show:

Morning routines lower cortisol (stress hormone) and boost mood stability.

Your Morning Mental Armor should include:

Silence Before Screens

No checking emails, news, or social media first thing.

Protect your mind before outside noise gets in.

Gratitude List (3 Things)

Proven to rewire the brain toward optimism and reduce depressive symptoms (University of California Berkeley).

Light Physical Movement

Walk

Stretch

Deep breathing for 3 minutes

Physical movement increases dopamine and serotonin—natural mood boosters.

Even a simple routine can be enough to shield your mind before the day attacks.

2. Midday Mental Check-In

By the middle of the day, stress, frustration, or anxiety can build up without you noticing.

The Mayo Clinic recommends scheduled emotional check-ins to stay ahead of overwhelm.

Midday tools:

Ask yourself: "How am I really doing right now?"

Step outside for 5 minutes of sunlight (proven to boost vitamin D and serotonin).

Practice 60 seconds of deep breathing or mindfulness.

Mental maintenance prevents mental meltdowns.

3. Evening Reset Ritual

How you end your day matters just as much as how you start it.

According to the Sleep Foundation:

People who develop calming evening routines experience better sleep quality and faster emotional recovery.

Your Reset Ritual could include:

Powering down screens 30–60 minutes before bed

Gentle stretching or meditation

Journaling three wins or moments of gratitude from the day

Reading something encouraging (instead of scrolling bad news).

Personally, I gave up reading or watching much news a few years ago, because it is purposely spun to be so negative. I know I may miss out on hearing about things when they first happen, but I must guard my mind.

There is also so much misinformation in the news these days. This way, when I do hear about something, I can do my own research about it to find out if it's true or not instead of being influenced by what the media and commercials want me to think about the world.

A good night's sleep isn't a luxury.

It's a weapon against depression and anxiety.

4. Weekly Maintenance Practices

In addition to daily habits, weekly "mental health maintenance" practices protect your long-term resilience.

Research shows that regular emotional hygiene routines lower the risk of major depressive episodes.

Weekly practices might include:

Therapy sessions (talk therapy, CBT, trauma therapy)

Support group meetings

Social connection with anchor people (even a coffee or a phone call)

Nature time (hiking, beach, parks — proven to lower stress hormones)

Creative outlets (painting, music, writing) for emotional processing

You maintain your car, your house, your health.

Why not your mind?

5. Build Flexibility Into Your Routine

Rigidity leads to guilt.

Guilt leads to giving up.

According to Psychology Today:

Flexible routines, not rigid ones, create the best long-term mental health outcomes.

On low days:

Shrink the routine.

Do 1% if you can't do 100%.

Survive the day, and rebuild tomorrow.

Flexibility isn't failure.

It's survival strategy.

Final Word on Routines

Daily routines don't cure mental illness.

But they give your mind structure when everything else feels unstable.

They give you habits to fall back on when motivation dies.

They give you victories you can count when your emotions lie to you.

Mind is the matter.

**And routines are how you keep
winning battles
every single day.**

Chapter 15: Break Glass
In Case of Emergency:
Your Crisis Survival Plan

No matter how strong you are, there will be days when everything crashes.

Days when your normal coping tools aren't enough.

Days when surviving the next hour feels impossible.

Those days are not a sign of failure.

They are part of the fight.

You need an Emergency Plan — something ready and real before the darkest moment hits.

According to the National Institute of Mental Health:

Having a crisis plan dramatically reduces the risk of self-harm, suicide attempts, and prolonged mental health crises.

This section builds that plan.

1. Pre-Program Emergency Contacts

On a crisis day, thinking clearly is almost impossible.

Action step:

Save at least three people in your phone under a label like "Emergency Anchor".

These must be people you trust to answer without judgment.

Tell them in advance:

"If you ever get a random call or text from me that just says HELP or SOS, know I need you."

Also save:

The National Suicide Prevention Lifeline (U.S.) — 988

Crisis Text Line — Text HOME to 741741

When you can't think straight, the numbers are already there.

2. Build a Crisis Environment

Your environment can make a huge difference on a crisis day.

Action step:

Have a physical "crisis kit" ready somewhere easy to reach.

Include:

A comforting blanket or hoodie

A note from yourself when you're feeling strong ("You will get through this. Don't believe the lies.")

Water and easy snacks (not alcohol)

A playlist of songs that have helped you survive

Fidget tools or stress balls (proven to help with anxiety attacks)

Change your surroundings.

Don't stay trapped in the place where the darkness hit.

3. Create a Crisis Action Card

According to Mental Health First Aid research:

Having a written action plan improves outcomes during mental health emergencies.

Write it out—short and simple.

Keep it somewhere you can grab when your brain isn't working right.

Example Crisis Action Card:

1. Drink water.

2. Call/text [Emergency Anchor Person].

3. Go outside and feel the air.

4. Play Safe Place Music.

5. Breathe — in for 4, out for 6, repeat 10 times.

6. Remind yourself: "This will not last forever."

7. If danger increases, call 988 or go to ER.

Make it so clear that even when you're broken, you can still follow it.

4. Use "One-Hour Survival Windows"

When life feels impossible, don't try to survive forever.

Just survive the next hour.

Psychological studies confirm:

Crisis emotions often peak and fade within 60–90 minutes.

Focus on surviving small windows:

Get through the next 5 minutes.

Then the next 15.

Then the next hour.

Stacking small survival windows gets you through until the chemicals in your brain settle.

> **"When you're going through hell, keep going."**
>
> **— Winston Churchill**

5. Emergency Reset Actions

If you're deep in a crisis spiral, do one of these immediate resets:

Splash ice water on your face (shocks the nervous system, slows panic).

Stand barefoot in grass, dirt, or sand (physical grounding).

Call someone and say out loud: "I need help right now."

Name out loud five things you can see around you (forces your brain into the present).

Don't trust your feelings during a crisis.

Trust your plan.

Final Word on Crisis Plans

Having an emergency plan doesn't mean you're weak.

It means you're smart enough to prepare for war before the battle hits.

You are not your worst day.

You are not your darkest thought.

You are not your crisis.

Mind is the matter.

And even on the days when your mind tries to destroy you

You still have weapons.

You still have choices.

You still have power.

Resources

National Alliance on Mental Illness
(NAMI) — nami.org

American Psychological Association
(APA) — apa.org

Mental Health America
(MHA) — mhanational.org

National Institute of Mental Health
(NIMH) — nimh.nih.gov

Crisis Text Line — Text HOME to 741741 or
visit crisistextline.org

National Suicide Prevention Lifeline
(U.S.) — Call 988

Mental Health First Aid USA —
mentalhealthfirstaid.org

Greater Good Science Center
(UC Berkeley) — greatergood.berkeley.edu

Harvard Medical School Mental Health Resources
health.harvard.edu

Psychology Today (Research & Articles) —
psychologytoday.com

References

American Foundation for Suicide Prevention. (2023). Suicide statistics. Retrieved from https://afsp.org/suicide-statistics

American Psychological Association. (2023). Understanding mental health and wellness. Retrieved from https://www.apa.org/topics/mental-health

Centers for Disease Control and Prevention. (2022). Connectedness: A strategic direction for suicide prevention. Retrieved from https://www.cdc.gov/suicide/pdf/connectedness.pdf

Crisis Text Line. (2023). Crisis services and emotional support. Retrieved from https://www.crisistextline.org

Greater Good Science Center. (2023). The science of happiness and resilience. Retrieved from https://greatergood.berkeley.edu

Harvard Medical School. (2023). The importance of routines in mental health. Retrieved from https://www.health.harvard.edu

Mental Health America. (2023). Living mentally healthy lives. Retrieved from https://www.mhanational.org

Mental Health First Aid USA. (2023). Mental Health First Aid curriculum and guidelines. Retrieved from https://www.mentalhealthfirstaid.org

National Alliance on Mental Illness. (2023). Mental health by the numbers. Retrieved from https://www.nami.org/mhstats

National Institute of Mental Health. (2023). Mental health information. Retrieved from https://www.nimh.nih.gov/health/statistics

Psychology Today. (2023). Strategies for emotional resilience and self-management. Retrieved from https://www.psychologytoday.com

Sleep Foundation. (2023). Healthy sleep habits and mental health. Retrieved from https://www.sleepfoundation.org

Acknowledgments

No battle is won alone.

This book exists because of the counselors who refused to give up on me when I had given up on myself.

To the doctors, therapists, friends, and family members who listened when I couldn't find the words — thank you for carrying the light when my world went dark.

To every person reading this book, struggling silently or fighting loudly:

You are stronger than your worst day.

You are braver than your darkest hour.

You are needed, and you are not alone.

Finally, to the version of myself who kept pushing forward even when it felt pointless — this one's for you.

Mind is the matter.

And you, my friend,
are proof that it matters enough to fight for.

www.ingramcontent.com/pod-product-compliance
Lightning Source LLC
Chambersburg PA
CBHW021145130626
46554CB00005B/1666